Real Estate Investing Flipping Houses for Profit

Complete beginner's Guide on How to Find, Finance, Rehab and Resell Homes in the right way for profit. Build-Up your Financial Freedom with this proven method.

By

Brandon Hammond

Table of Contents

Introduction 7

Chapter 1: The Basics of Property Flipping 12

Chapter 2: Creating your Network 19

   A Licensed Real Estate Agent 19

      Submit Offers to Purchase a Property 20

      Presenting the CMAs 21

      Determining Your ARV 22

      Locate the Buyers 23

   A Real Estate Appraiser 28

   The Lender 29

   Title Companies 30

Chapter 3: Real Estate Market and How the National Economy 32

   The Interest Rates on Mortgages 34

   The Current Lending Requirements 36

   The Unemployment Rates 37

      Know the Market Area 38

   The Local Economic Growth and Stability 39

   The Local Activity in Regards to Real Estate 41

Chapter 4: Understanding the Buyer in Your Local Market 45

What Does the Buyer Want?... 46

What Things Do Buyers Not Like? 50

Location is Important to Your Buyers... 52

Chapter 5: Getting the Financing Your Investment Needs to Get off the Ground 55

Conventional Financing 56

Hard Money Loans 58

Work With a HELOC... 60

Owner Financing... 61

Getting Yourself Prepared for Financing 64

Chapter 6: Choosing the Property You Want to Flip and Make a Profit From 67

It Meets the Requirements of the Buyer... 69

Learn What the True Market Value of the Property Is... 73

What is the Seller's Motivation 78

The Three Very Important Rules 80

A Note About Trulia and Zillow 82

Chapter 7: The Steps to Purchase Your First Property to Flip... 86

The Purchase Agreement 86

The Purchase Price 88

Safety Clauses.. 89

Earnest Money Deposit 91

The Inspection 92

    Who to Bring 92

    What to Bring 93

    Where to Look... 95

    When You Should Run Away 97

Chapter 8: Working on a Quick Flip to Make Money in Property Flipping Today! 100

Finding the Right Property 100

Change the Look for Cheap 102

Make Money with Property Flipping Without a Lot of Rehab 104

Chapter 9: Doing Property Flipping with a Renovation Property..107

How to Find One of These Properties 107

How to Determine How Profitable the Property Will Be 109

    The Purchase Price 110

    The Rehab 110

    The After Repair Value..113

Doing it Yourself or Hiring a Contractor 114

How to Manage Your Rehab 117

Chapter 10: How to Sell Your Property and Make a Profit 120

Selling on Your Own or Selling with an Agent? 120

Attracting Buyers to Your House 123

Advertising *123*

Staging *125*

Open Houses *126*

Land Contracts and Lease Options *126*

Do I Want to Rent Out My Property? 129

Chapter 11: Challenges That Come with Your First Property Flip and Beyond 132

Your ARV is Always Changing 133

The Tax Implications 133

A Lengthy Holding Period 135

Lack of Experience 136

Not All Property Flips Are Going to Be Profitable 137

Chapter 12: Tips That Will Help Reduce Your Risks and Help You Make Maximum Profit on Your Flip 139

Watch Your Time Versus the Money You Make 139

Make Sure That You Don't Run out of Money 141

Under Build Rather Than Overbuild 142

Remember to Factor in Those Holding Costs 143

Choose the Property That Is the Best Investment, Not the First Property You See 145

Develop Your Own System 148

Be Patient.. 149

Try to Sell the House on Your Own 151

Make Your Estimates for Repairs Higher Than You Think 152

Chapter 13: A Review of Property Flipping and How to Get Started 155

Conclusion 160

© Copyright 2018 by __Brandon Hammond__ - All rights reserved.

The following eBook is reproduced below with the goal of providing information that is as accurate and reliable as possible. Regardless, purchasing this eBook can be seen as consent to the fact that both the publisher and the author of this book are in no way experts on the topics discussed within and that any recommendations or suggestions that are made herein are for entertainment purposes only. Professionals should be consulted as needed prior to undertaking any of the action endorsed herein.

This declaration is deemed fair and valid by both the American Bar Association and the Committee of Publishers Association and is legally binding throughout the United States.

Furthermore, the transmission, duplication, or reproduction of any of the following work including specific information will be considered an illegal act irrespective of if it is done electronically or in print. This extends to creating a secondary or tertiary copy of the work or a recorded copy and is only allowed with the express written consent from the Publisher. All additional rights reserved.

The information in the following pages is broadly considered a truthful and accurate account of facts and as such, any inattention, use, or misuse of the information in question by the reader will render any resulting actions solely under their purview. There are no scenarios in which the publisher or the original author of this work can be in any fashion deemed liable for any hardship or damages that may befall them after undertaking information described herein.

Additionally, the information in the following pages is intended only for informational purposes and should thus be thought of as universal. As befitting its nature, it is presented without assurance regarding its prolonged validity or interim quality. Trademarks that are mentioned are done without written consent and can in no way be considered an endorsement from the trademark holder.

Introduction

Congratulations on downloading *Real Estate Investing—Flipping Houses for Profit* and thank you for doing so.

The following chapters will discuss all the steps you need to know to get into the world of property flipping. Property flipping is simply the idea that you purchase a property, below market value, do some fixes and repairs on it before selling the property for a profit. Sounds simple right? While the steps may seem pretty straightforward here, there is a lot that goes into property flipping and if you don't take the time to research the market, pick the right property, figure out your costs, and sell the house quickly, it could end up costing you a lot of money.

This guidebook will discuss everything you need to know to get started in property flipping and real estate investing. You will learn how to research the market, find the right financing, and even how to get that house bought, fixed, and sold in no time. This can be a lengthy and busy process, but for those who understand how this investment works, and who are willing to put the time and effort in, it can be very rewarding as well.

When you are ready to start investing your money into real estate and seeing some of the amazing results that you can get with growing your money, make sure to check out this guidebook to get started!

There are plenty of books on this subject on the market, thanks again for choosing this one! Every effort was made to ensure it is full of as much useful information as possible, please enjoy!

Chapter 1: The Basics of Property Flipping

Most people are introduced to the idea of property flipping from reality television. They see people who are able to drop money on a house that is pretty much falling apart, do a few improvements, and then make a lot of money in a few months. While these television shows do tend to glamorize the idea of house flipping, property flipping is still a legitimate way to make money and an investment in your future. You simply need to know how to do it and the right steps to take, and you could make this a full-time income.

The first step here is to learn exactly what property flipping is all about. Property flipping is defined as the buying and selling of a house, all in the same calendar year. So technically, if you purchase a house for personal use and then have to move out of state ten months later, you would be property flipping. Most of the time, property flipping is going to occur when an investor purchases a property and then turns around and sells it within the next year to make a profit. This can include repair and renovation to help the investor make a profit on reselling that property.

There are a few basic methods involved when it comes to making money when you flip a house. These include:

The quick flip: For this method, the investor is going to locate a house that is below its market value. The investor would then purchase the house and do a few quick repairs. They want to do as little as possible to increase the value in a short amount of time. They may fix a few items, apply some new paint, or do some update to the appeal of the house. Within a few months, sometimes even shorter, the investor will resell the house back at market value and take the profits.

The renovation: With this option, the investor is going to locate a house that needs quite a few repairs, rehabilitation, or some modernization. The house is purchased and then over a few months, the investor will renovate it to maximize the market value. The investor will get a profit simply by subtracting the original price along with the selling costs and the costs of repairs from the price that they sell the house for.

How Can I Make Money Flipping Houses?

Looking at the above, it may seem pretty simple to make some money from flipping houses. There is a lot of money that you can make when you flip houses, but you have to be careful. Those who jump in too quickly without doing their research, or who spend too much on a house or its repairs, will end up losing money in the process. Some of the things that you need to know before you can make money flipping houses include:

- You need to have a feel for the pulse of the market: You need to know how high the demand is for buyers in that area, as well as the amount that the buyers are willing to pay.

- o If the investor pays $100,000 for a house, and then another $30,000 renovating the kitchen to get it ready for the sale, but the buyers will only pay $115,000 in that market, the investor would lose $15,000 in the process.

- The investor needs to be able to come up with accurate estimates for repairs. You might be able to find a house that is offered at a good price, but if your repairs end up being way more than you planned, then you can lose out on money. Even those who are more experienced with contracting will admit that sometimes it is hard to know how much renovation is needed until you get started.

    - o If you budget $10,000 to renovate your kitchen, then get into the work and find that the wiring is below standard, and the subfloor is rotten, you may have to pay more. You might end up paying $15,500 for that. If this puts you above market value for the house, you will lose money.

- You need to have an accurate estimate of the After Repair Value of the house before you start on the rehab: The success of property flipping is going to rely on how much you can sell the house for. And the quality and the amount of the renovations that you want to do will hinge on this number as well.

    o When you worked with an agent, you were going to purchase a house for $125,000 with the assumption that it will sell for $165,000. After spending about $25,000 on repairs and then paying for the closing costs, you estimated you would earn $15,000. But wait, the agent overestimated the property's value and you were only able to make $148,000 when you sold the house. This results in a loss of all the profit and $2000 extra out of pocket.

This is not meant to scare you away from getting into the market for flipping houses. It is simply there to show you that being successful with it can be hard for some people, and takes some research and hard work. If you do the calculations the wrong way, you may end up getting a big financial loss.

So, it is possible to make money when you choose to flip houses, you just need to make sure that you know what you are doing and not just jump in and hope that it all goes well. You need to study the market, have a good idea of what a potential buyer is looking for, have the right tools to measure the profitability of your project, and the endurance to get it all done and sell the property. It is a great investment that can make you a lot of money, but it also comes with a lot of work in the process.

Although property flipping is not really as active now as it was in the past before the recent downturn economy and the foreclosures that came with it, there is still a great market for this niche. According to RealtyTrac, house flips were able to make up about 4.5 percent of house sales during the second quarter of 2015. Even though this is a lower number, the return on investment jumped up from 24 percent to 36 percent compared to the past year.

It is possible to flip a house, but you need to do your research, have a good team, and be prepared to take on any challenge that comes up with this investment. If you can put all of this together and you can put in the hard work, you are going to see this investment work well for you.

Chapter 2: Creating your Network

While the reality television portray the property flipper as someone who does all the work on their own, this is simply not reality. In order to have a successful property flip, you must have a team of professionals on your side. They will be able to help you find a good deal, get the paperwork filed, find the properties, fix up the properties, and even sell them when you are ready. Before you even start to analyze the deals on the market and submitting the offers, make sure you have a good network of people behind you first. Some of the professionals that you need to make your property flipping investment a success includes:

A Licensed Real Estate Agent

One of the first people you should search to have on your team is a qualified real estate agent. Some property flippers decide that they are not going to purchase their property off the MLS, or Multiple Listing Service, so they assume they do not need a real estate agent at all. However, these agents have a wealth of knowledge about the market you are in, they know a lot of people, and they will be a very valuable resource when you are getting into this market. Some of the different services that your real estate agent can provide you, whether you plan to use the MLS or not, include:

Submit Offers to Purchase a Property

Real estate agents are trained to be good negotiators. Their purchase agreements are designed in a way to be legally protective of you as the purchaser. Additionally, they can take on some other tasks such as preparing, submitting, and tracking how your offer does. This can really free up some of your time, especially if you have another job or are looking at multiple properties at once.

The good news is that the buyer's agent is free. The seller is the one who will pay for the services of the real estate agent, so this is a great tool to use. The real estate agent gets paid as long as you purchase a property, but you don't have to worry about money out of your pocket when you purchase the property.

Presenting the CMAs

As a new investor, do you really have the time, resources, or training to really track all of the properties that have recently sold in your market? If you are in a small town, you might be able to try doing this. But if you are in a big city, which is where a lot of your potential properties will be, the recently sold properties in your area over the past year could be thousands. A good real estate agent is going to have all this information stored in their database and they could help you out with a good CMA, or Comparative Market Analysis, to make things easier.

The reason why you want to work with a CMA is to help you come up with the most likely sales price for any property. You would get this number by comparing, and making adjustments when needed, recent sales that were similar in that neighborhood. So, if you are looking at a property that is three bedrooms, two baths, you would look at other houses that sold in the past year that had three bedrooms and two baths and were about the same square footage and land space. You would not compare to a house that has five bedrooms, three baths, and ten acres because the prices would be way different.

When you take the time to combine the experience form your agent with the knowledge that comes from this data, you are going to have a great resource that will help you get the right price for a property while also making a profit.

Determining Your ARV

First, you may be asking what the ARV is all about. This stands for "After Renovation Value." It is the sales price that is most likely for your property after you take some time to repair, remodel, and renovate it. This is a very critical number for you to concentrate on because all your profits, calculations, and estimates are going to be based on it. If you are really off on the number, especially if you aim too high in the number, you could end up in debt from this venture. You never want to guess or be wrong on this. If you aren't positive in your own ability to do this, find a professional, such as your real estate agent, who can prepare the numbers for you.

Locate the Buyers

After you have taken the time to do all the renovations on the house and gotten it to look better, you will be ready to sell. And the faster that you can sell the property, the more profits you will make. Each month that you hold onto the property results in more taxes, more principal and interest payments, and more money out of your own pocket. Your real estate agent can help you find the right buyers as quickly as possible. Factor in their commissions when doing your numbers so you don't end up with a surprise at the end. But it is usually worth your time to let the real estate agent do the legwork and sell the property for you when you're done.

Licensed Contractors

Unless you have your own contractor's license and the right skills and experience to rehab a house (which most beginners in property flipping will not have), then you need to add a good contractor to your time. Not only will they help out with some, or all, of your project, but they can provide you with an initial inspection of the property and you can use their comments about that property to determine how much it will cost to fix and whether that property is a good investment.

You may find as you grow your investment that you need several different contractors to help get the house ready. In the beginning though, just network with a general contractor. They will be able to help you get started and can easily recommend others to you as needed. If you are uncertain about how to find a general contractor, a good place to start is to ask your real estate agent.

When you are working on property flipping and you need to renovate the house, you want the work to be done right the first time. This saves time and a lot of money. Finding the right contractor who can do this can sometimes be the hardest part of your job.

The first rule is to stay away from any contractors who are more handymen than anything else. These are the contractors who do the work on the side to make a little extra rather than the ones who do it all the time as a professional. These handymen may not be insured or licensed so even if they do save you money, their work can look bad and if something goes wrong with what they do, you won't have much recourse to work with.

It is important to go with a contractor who is insured, bonded, and licensed and who have a lot of experience in their fields. This may cost you a bit more upfront, but on the long run, it can help you. It ensures that the work is done right the first time, so you aren't repaying to get the work done and losing out on valuable time. These professionals also do higher quality of work, which can really impress your buyers when it comes to selling.

A House Inspector

When you are ready to sell your property, the buyer is almost always going to hire a house inspector. This inspector is going to take a look all around the property and then prepare a report to the buyer. The buyer can then request to get certain things fixed or changed in the property before they purchase. Sometimes these are little things, such as fix a leak in a drain that the inspector noticed, and other times it could be something big, like fix the furnace.

You can use a house inspector as well. First, you can offer that inspector as someone the buyer can use if they are looking for references. You can also use it for the purchase property inspection. Even though you will also have a contractor on your team, the property inspector is going to be useful as well. A complete inspection costs a bit of money out of pocket, but it can really save you.

They may find a big issue that needs to be fixed before you can sell the house again, and the cost of that may put you over budget. Knowing this ahead of time can get you out of the house before any contracts are signed or before you are stuck. On the other side, the inspector may find that the house only needs a little bit of cosmetic work before being good to go, and you may be able to do the work on your own rather than hiring a contractor on that property.

You may also need to use an inspector to help out with your pre-sale inspection. If the buyer comes in with an inspector and receives a list of 30 things that need to be fixed, even if they are little things, they may think the house is not worth as much as you are selling it for, and the sale may flop. Having that inspector come in and look over the property can ensure that you catch these things and that the buyer feels they are getting the most out of their money.

A Real Estate Appraiser

Usually, the appraiser is only going to come into the picture when a buyer is getting bank financing and the lender will hire this professional to make sure the house is really worth what the buyer is going to pay. However, there may be some projects you work on that are complex and you may want another professional to come in, rather than just relying on the CMA, to help you make a good decision on the property.

The appraiser is going to be your expert in valuation. They are going to apply a broader range of value tests than a real estate agent can. They also have a greater degree of technical knowledge and they are required by law to have E&O insurance. This individual can help you know how much the house is worth, how a specific renovation will change the value of the house and more.

The Lender

If you want to start flipping properties full time, then you need to have a good relationship with at least two lenders in your area. You can technically choose any lender that you would like, but local banks and credit unions are often best. The bigger national chains of banks are not happy when they are asked for short-term loans, like the one you will need in property flipping. But the credit unions and community banks will have less stringent loan criteria, and they are open to helping you out with this loan.

This is also the time when you should explore the various financing options available. Property flippers will generally average about six months before they are able to turn around and sell their property. You will need financing to help you not only purchase the house but to help with all the repairs and renovations along the way.

Having a good relationship with the right lender can really make the process go faster in the future.

Title Companies

The title company can be useful when you are handling all the aspects of a closing. You can choose to work with an attorney, but most buyers and sellers feel more comfortable working with a title company. To start, they are cheaper and their in-house attorneys are able to put together all the paperwork that you need for that property.

These title companies can be useful in other situations as well. If you want to do a title search on a property, they are there to help. If you ever plan to research an abandoned House, a property that is in foreclosure, or properties with more than one owner in common, then you will want the title company to help.

Having this team of professionals to help you out during property flipping can really make the transaction go smoothly. These individuals and professionals have a lot of experience and the tools that you need to help see success. Treat them with respect and find the ones that you can rely on, and you are going to be on your way to making money in real estate in no time.

Chapter 3: Real Estate Market and How the National Economy

No matter which market you decide to enter, there are a lot of factors going on that will determine the price of houses in your area, the price of getting work done, and how much you can make when you get into property flipping. Even the state of the national economy can determine how well property flipping can go, no matter how far from D.C. you may be.

Remember the housing crisis that occurred from 2007 to 2010? While the effects didn't happen in all parts of the country at once, it did have a profound effect on the real estate market and how many people were purchasing houses. According to Alan Greenspan, the former Chairman of the Federal Reserve, the United States did not experience a nationwide housing bubble necessarily, but a number of more local bubbles. He was then quoted as saying in 2007 "all the froth bubbles add up to an aggregate bubble."

When the housing crisis happened, many people were losing their houses. They had spent too much on the property and either lost their jobs or they were making mortgage payments that they couldn't afford. The housing market had really inflated the prices of houses, which was temporarily a great thing for investors who were able to purchase a house and, with very few changes, sell it for a big profit a little bit later. But this inflation, and lax lending practices, meant that many people owned houses they couldn't afford and foreclosures became very prevalent.

It took some time for the market to recover and for some time, many houses were not being sold. And the ones that were being sold were sold at a loss. Many houses that had been overinflated were now being sold off for much less, and because of fear of the market, there weren't that many buyers available.

A property flipper can be affected on both sides of this example. When the housing market was going crazy and some house prices seemed to double overnight, they were able to find many properties and make a profit on them in no time. But once the market crashed, they had a hard time finding any buyers for any properties they purchased.

This is just one example of how important it is to look not only at the market in your area for real estate, but also the national economy and other factors to determine which property is right and whether you are getting a good deal on a property. Some of the other factors that a property flipper should consider when they want to make a purchase include:

The Interest Rates on Mortgages

The interest rates for mortgages throughout the nation are going to have a direct correlation to the buying and selling of real estate. Lower interest rates are nice because they will encourage more first time house buyers to stop renting and purchase their own house instead. It can even be a motivating factor for some current house buyers to upgrade and move to a house that is more luxurious and larger.

However, there are times when the mortgage rates are going to go up. When these rates increase, you will find that the activity in real estate is going to slow down and decrease. This doesn't mean there won't be any interested buyers, but there will be fewer than before. The raising of interest rates for a mortgage can easily affect the number of willing buyers for a property.

Knowing where the national mortgage rates are when you enter the market can be important. If they are low, this means the demand for houses is higher and you can make more of a profit. When the rates are lower, you can still make a profit, but you may need to be more selective with the properties you choose to flip.

The Current Lending Requirements

Ever since the housing crisis occurred, the federal government has really cracked down on risky, interest-only loans to borrowers who are not in good standing. This does cut down a bit on how many buyers are on the market for your property but helps to protect the banks from a defaulting loan.

As a property flipper, you need to keep ahead of any current lending requirements. In some cases, it can help you keep focus better when you are doing your renovations. It can also help you to tailor your marketing to those who are the most likely to qualify for a mortgage to purchase your house.

In some cases, such as when the mortgage guidelines get really tight, you could consider doing something like owner financing. This can maximize your return. If the buyer isn't able to purchase the property, you get to keep some of the money they paid ahead. But if they can pay it at the end of the term, you get to sell the house because there were more interested buyers on the market.

Each bank is going to have their own rules when it comes to lending as well. This is another reason why it may be a good idea to go with a local credit union or bank. These options often want to support the local community and can give out more loans compared to some of the bigger names in the industry. Check to see what some of the local rules for mortgages are in your area and determine how that will affect your business.

The Unemployment Rates

You should look at the rates of unemployment both in your area and nationally. These employment rates will help you measure the health of the national economy. When unemployment is low, this is a good thing for you. This means there are more jobs in your area and that people have money to spend on houses. But if there is a sharp rise in unemployment, it could mean that you have fewer potential buyers and will need to spend more time marketing any properties you want to sell.

Know the Market Area

While it is very important for you to watch the mortgage terms, the economic indicators, the interest rates, and employment trends nationally, you will also want to pay attention to what is going on in your own market, or the market you wish to buy and sell in. It is critical to always pay attention to the local housing market, because sometimes it is different than what you see nationally. For example, the nation may have great unemployment rates, but a big factory in your market just closed down and people don't have jobs to purchase a house. Without having a good idea of what is going on in the real estate market near you, you can risk tens of thousands, or even more, in the process.

The Local Economic Growth and Stability

One of the things that you need to look into when understanding your market area is having a good understanding of the local economy. And the best way to do this is to be very familiar with the Planning and Zoning office. Pay particular attention to any announcements of new developments or some proposed construction in your area. This gives you a good indication of where the real estate market is going in your area.

For example, if you take the time to attend any of the public planning and zoning meetings in your area, you may find out that they approved a large shopping mall that is going to be built near the edge of town. This lets you know that at some point, buyers are going to start looking for places to live out near that same area. You could get a jump on the game and see if there are any reasonable properties, perhaps some which need a little work, that is within five minutes of where the new mall is rising.

It can work the other way for you too. If you are searching through your local paper and see that one of the major employers from the area is running into some financial problems, and they have already started to lay off some of their employees. This isn't going to make the residents of the area feel like they are secure in their jobs and none of them are really thinking about purchasing a house soon. You may want to take a break here and look at other nearby markets instead of selling there.

This can also work the other way for you as an investor. If you find that a new factory is coming to the area, or another business that can offer some good jobs, then it may be time to purchase some properties, especially if that area has cheap housing. As soon as news about that new business shows up and they start hiring, people will move to the area, people will have more money, and the prices of real estate will go up, giving you a nice profit.

Depending on which property you picked, you may not even need to do a ton of work on the property either!

The Local Activity in Regards to Real Estate

This is an example of where you would use a real estate agent to help you out. They are able to gather all the data up for you and then help you measure it and figure out how to understand what is going on with the real estate market in your area.

Before you head over and talk with your real estate agent with some generic questions, why not come up with a list of questions that you would like to know about ahead of time? This allows the agent time to look up the information that you need and sets them up to answer your questions a little bit better. Some of the questions that you can consider asking if you are not sure where to start include:

- What percentage of the houses that are listed are REO's? What discount do these properties end up receiving usually? Some property flippers decide to purchase bank repossessions or REOs. This helps them to get a property below market value in some cases. Buying a property from a bank is a long and boring process and they often end up selling the property "as is." Even when a problem is found, they don't want to lower the price. And in some cases, you may be on a limit for how much you can resell the property for. If you see that the listed REOs are discounted less than ten percent, then move on to another option.

- How much are houses selling on average in the area? If you notice that more than sixty percent of the houses sold in the last year ranged between $145,000 and $175,000, then it is probably not reasonable to find a house for $50,000 that you could sell for $200,000.

- What are the average days on market for the main price categories? This helps you to have an idea of how long you could potentially hold onto the property, and you can factor this into your own costs.

- What types of properties seem to sell the fastest in this market? If you and your agent are able to narrow down which properties are able to see the fastest, then it is much easier for you to figure out what the buyers want out of a house. Do you see some houses that the buyers purchase quickly that are similar in sizes, layouts, and features? Are they all found in the same area?

- Which neighborhoods seem to have the most activity: While you may be fond of one area of town, the typical buyer may or may not agree with you. If you find that the typical buyer likes another area of town, then that is where you need to look for houses.

Understanding your local market can make a big difference in how much you spend on a property, how long you hold onto that property, and even what types of renovations you decide to do. Knowing the market, both naturally and locally, can help you get started and will reduce your risk of losing money on this investment by quite a bit.

Chapter 4: Understanding the Buyer in Your Local Market

Another thing that you need to consider when you want to sell a house is the buyer of that property. It doesn't matter what house you purchase, or how long you renovate a house, if you can't sell that property, you are going to go broke. So, before you even decide to take the time to look for the right properties to flip, you need to have a good understanding of your buyer and what they are looking for when they purchase a house.

Here is another conversation that you can have with your real estate agent. They know a lot of people in the market and may be able to provide you with some information that you couldn't find elsewhere. Offer to buy them lunch and spend some time on this topic. You want to know exactly where the buyer market activity is coming from because it will really affect the type of property you purchase and what renovations you do to it. Some of the questions you can discuss with your agent during this time include:

Are the buyers in this market young families, retirees, working professionals or another group?

What neighborhoods seem to appeal the most to each different buying group?

Are you seeing more buyers getting mortgages or paying cash? Are they getting the traditional mortgages through a bank or are they interested in different options like owner financing?

What type of house is each buying category the most interested in?

What Does the Buyer Want?

Once you take some time to learn more about who is purchasing houses in your area, it is time to narrow down what these particular buyers are looking for when they purchase a new house. If you can purchase a house and then change it to meet the top needs of a buyer, along with a few of their wants, you can get a competitive price in no time. Depending on the market, doing this could get you several offers, which can drive your final price up.

Each buyer is a bit different in what they want to get out of the house, but some of the most popular things they want to see include:

- Baths and kitchens that are updated: Young buyers are going to want a new kitchen. They don't have the money to put into a new kitchen because they put most of their savings into furnishings for the house and the down payment. This leaves nothing for them to spend on remodelling on their own. New bath fixtures are just as important and can dramatically increase the appeal of the house. These can get expensive though so make sure you watch what is going on and keep a good budget with these repairs.

- An open eat-in kitchen: The formal dining rooms and the open up kitchens are a thing of the past. The kitchen is now a hangout room for families and for entertainment. If you are already redoing the kitchen, you should consider turning it into an eat-in, if possible, because these are really in demand right now, especially with families who have children.

- Exterior lighting: You need to have plenty of exterior lighting to impress buyers. These can include landscape accent lights, ground spotlights, and wall lanterns. These can make a great first impression and do wonders when it comes to curb appeal.

- Separate laundry room: Many buyers want to see a separate laundry room with an area for ironing and folding clothes. A recent study says that this is important for up to 93 percent of current buyers.

- Open floor plan: There are many buyers who seem to enjoy the open floor plan. If there are simple ways for you to open up the floor plan a bit, then this is what you should do.

- House office: Many young buyers are currently working from home, at least a few days a week. Having a house office is important for them.

- Walk-in pantries: In one recent study, about 85 percent of buyers would prefer if their new house had a walk-in pantry that would have enough room to not only store food, but also brooms and mops.

- Low maintenance turnkey houses: Many buyers want to make sure that they get into a house that won't need a lot of work on it. This is especially important when it comes to the flooring and landscaping. Go with an option like wood floors and some granite countertops to entice your buyer.

- Energy efficiency: Many young buyers are happy to go green and are energy conscience. Buyers may not pay more for these, but if you already have to purchase new appliances for the house, make sure to get ones that are Energy Star rated.

Remember that every buyer is going to be a little bit different. They will have specific things they want in their new house. You can talk with a real estate agent to see which types of features are really popular in your market so you get them included in your property. Adding in that little extra will help you to really impress the buyers and will get the property off the market quickly.

What Things Do Buyers Not Like?

While there are some preferences that many buyers would like to have in their new houses, there are also some features that will turn them off a house and can make it hard to sell that house. If you purchase a property that already has some of these factors, you should try to change them out, even if they are in good condition.

- Finished ceilings that look like popcorn: This was a popular style in the 80s, but most buyers do not like the look now. Scrape these off and sell the house with a smooth ceiling.

- Brass fixtures: These are things found in really old houses, and many buyers want some modern touches in the house.

- Vanity strip bathroom lighting: Your potential buyer doesn't want to be blinded by these lights or feel like they are in a dressing room. Replace these lights with something better.

- Lack of storage: Storage is so important when it comes to the property. The more storage your property has, the better it is. Add in a few cabinets and shelves to help fix this problem if it is there for your property.

- Tight houses: Buyers don't like to be in houses that have small compartmentalized rooms. They like the open floor plan. But before you go through and bust out some walls, make sure that you get a contractor there to ensure the right walls are being removed.

It is just as important for you as a property flipper to avoid the things that buyers don't like. If these things show up in your house, you may find that some buyers won't be interested in purchasing the house at all, and your property may stay on the market way too long. When thinking about the renovations that you want to do on the house, check on these topics to get them fixed before you try to sell the property.

Location is Important to Your Buyers

The house can follow all of the other suggestions in this chapter, but if it is found in the wrong location, it is going to be hard to find the right buyer. The location of your property is going to be a big factor in whether a buyer will purchase the house or not. You can talk to your agent to figure out whether buyers seem to be preferring the suburbs or downtown.

The type of buyer you are aiming for will make a difference in the location you want to purchase. If you are trying to market to families, you want to pick out properties in safer locations, such as those near parks and schools. Many buyers are also interested in a house that is close to any public transportation area and that have a good walk score. You can also look for houses that are close to dining, recreation, entertainment, and shopping.

Another area that you can focus on is any neighborhoods that you may want to consider is one that is undergoing a rejuvenation. This could be through an investment by that city or because others purchased houses there and are fixing them up. This area can offer you with lower-priced houses, but since the area is getting fixed up, the demand for the houses will soon go up and you can make a good profit.

Preparing for your buyer is an important step in the property flipping process. There are a lot of different types of properties that you can choose to purchase, but not all of them will make you a profit or attract the kind of buyer that you want. Understanding that buyer, and following some of the tips in this chapter, will ensure that you are going to find someone who is willing to purchase your property so you make an income.

Chapter 5: Getting the Financing Your Investment Needs to Get off the Ground

Once you have done a little bit of research about the market in your area, it is time to focus on purchasing the first property for flipping. Some investors will choose to pay all cash for the property. But most new investors in property flipping will not have the cash around to do this and they will need to rely on financing to help them out.

Obtaining conventional financing as a property investor can be hard on its own, but getting this kind of loan for a short-term period is almost impossible. As a property flipper, you won't need or want the 30-year traditional mortgage loan because you don't plan to hold onto the property for that long. You usually only need your financing for about 12 months or less, and the target here is for less than six minutes.

National lenders will make the most money on the idea that they can sell loans to the secondary mortgage market, and some companies, such as Freddie Mac and Fannie Mae, are only interested in doing the long-term loans. Thus, in order to obtain the conventional financing for this investment, you will need to work with a lender who is willing to hold the loans in-house.

Getting financing can be hard for this kind of endeavor, but you have to find it somewhere since having the house is a pretty big expense. Let's take a look at some of the different options that you can choose when it comes to financing your property flip.

Conventional Financing

The method that is considered the safest when it comes to paying for a property flip, outside of having the cash outright to pay for the property, is to get conventional financing. The in-house loans, which are easier to get for this option, are going to be backed by the equity in the house along with your own personal creditworthiness, rather than in the equity of the house. A good place to start when you are doing this is to visit local banks and credit unions. These options are more likely to write out short-term portfolio loans to fund your purchases.

To help you qualify for these loans, you need to meet some pretty strict lending requirements, and you will probably have to come up with a large down payment. You need to have a score that is at least 620, but since this kind of investing is a little bit riskier than other types of mortgages, you will probably need to have a credit score that is at least in the 700s.

When you are looking for a lender, it is a good idea to shop around for a bit. Be upfront with the lender about what you would like to do with the money and how you plan to go about making money and paying it back. You need to be prepared as much as possible, showing your experience, what you would do with the money and more makes it easier to get a lender to work with you on this investment.

If you do decide that you want to go with a conventional loan, make sure that the rates are reasonable and won't cost you too much out of your profit. You also want to check that there isn't a prepayment penalty. Many conventional loans can carry a restriction on when you are able to resell the property. But if you talk this over with your lender, you may be able to get a loan that will lift this penalty so you don't have to pay those out later.

Hard Money Loans

Another option that you can go with is a hard money loan. These are short-term, non-bank loans that are given out to either a private investor or a company. The loan does have a guarantee that is more on the value of the chosen property rather than on the credit of the borrower. Savvy investors will use these kinds of loans all of the time and they are excellent options to use when you are doing a property flip.

When you know exactly what you are getting into with your investor and you can add in the higher than average loan costs to the formula, these hard money loans can be great for you. However, you do need to weigh the risks of going with one of these because while they are great options, there are times when they could cost you a lot of money.

Working with a hard money loan can be really expensive and you need to factor these expenses into your profitability calculations. These lenders are going to charge a very high interest rate, usually at least fourteen percent, and they can carry multiple points and have high closing costs. Points are going to be paid up front with each point being about one percent of the loan amount. This can cost you a bit more upfront, but it does help when you need a quick short-term loan to finance the investment.

The loans that you get from this are going to be made based on the after repair value of the house and they are going to have a loan to value ratio between 55 and 75 percent based on the borrower's credit score. This can pick up any purchase equity and can include some funding for repairs.

Work With a HELOC

Do you have a personal residence or some other investment property of your own that has some equity? If you do, then you may want to take this equity and use a House Equity Line of Credit, or a HELOC, to help you fund your endeavor. This is a better option than an Equity Loan because this amount is more like a credit card limit rather than a bank loan. You can borrow up to the maximum loan amount, pay it back, and then borrow again without having to worry about going through the lending process each time. These loans will only allow you to take out a maximum total loan to value of 80 percent, which will include your first mortgage and the HELOC.

So, if your house is worth $250,000 and you have a mortgage on it for $145,000, the maximum amount that you would be able to pull out using a HELOC for $55,000. This may not cover the whole amount of the purchase unless you have a lot of equity, but it does help you get money for some repairs if needed.

The interest rate on these are going to be higher than what you get with a conventional mortgage, but your closing costs are going to be lower. But, if you borrow against the equity that is in your personal residence, and the investment property doesn't go well, you need to make sure there is enough money left over in your regular monthly budget to cover that additional amount you now owe on the loan.

Owner Financing

Purchasing a property on a land contract, which is often known as owner financing, can be a good way to finance your short-term purchase. There are some property owners out there who don't mind doing this because it helps them to earn a little bit extra on the sale of their house. This leads to you getting what you want, and the seller getting what they want.

For this option, instead of working to get a conventional mortgage, you would instead make monthly payments to the person who owns the property now. You would have to come up with a down payment at the time that you close, but this is often less than ten percent. The owner will be able to charge interest as well, setting it about one or two percentage points above the conventional mortgage rates, but sometimes they may consider setting it higher. When you are ready to resell the property, you will pay off the remainder of the loan balance and you can keep the profit.

If you need financing but you don't have a good down payment, this may be an option for you. The owner would simply carry the mortgage on the property in the second position, with the conventional financing they have as the first. You would still need to figure out how you would pay for the repairs, and you would need to find a seller who is willing to do this.

Another option with the use of owner financing is to purchase the property "Subject TO" the existing mortgage. The buyer is going to pay the seller the difference between the purchase price and the balance the seller has on the mortgage at that time. Then they will take over the payments that are left on the seller's mortgage. There are usually clauses in the contract that are against this for mortgage companies, but the lender may be willing to overlook this as long as the payment is done on time.

The house-owner may not like this option because it is a risk. From their perspective, you could easily agree to do this and then not make the payments on time. This would end up harming the house-owner's credit score. In most cases, the sellers who are quick to take this offer are the ones who are already behind on their mortgage payments and are worried about foreclosure.

Getting Yourself Prepared for Financing

Part of your success in getting a loan is going to be dependent on your creditworthiness. The other part is based on how well you know what you are doing. If you just go in and say you want the money to purchase a property and make a lot of money, the bank is going to turn you down. If you go in with a clear understanding of exactly how much you need, exactly what you are going to spend it on, and all the costs and risks of the endeavor, then you are more likely to get the money.

Once you have taken the time to decide on the kind of financing that you would like, and you are either pre-qualified or pre-approved, you will need to provide your lender with some more proof. This will include a lot of documents, including the purchase agreement for the house, the contract that you have with your contractor, at least two estimates of renovation costs, a marketing plan, the anticipated holding costs, and the projected time to get it all done.

The more information that you are able to provide to the bank, the better off it will be. This shows them that you aren't just rushing in hoping to make it big. The bank, or any other lender, would want to make sure that you are prepared and that they will actually earn their money back if they lend it to you, especially on such a short-term loan.

Not only will you need to provide the bank with all this information, but the lender is going to have a lot of hard questions for you to answer. Some of these questions include:

- How much past experience do you have working on similar projects?
  How much of your personal funds do you plan to use on this property flip?

- What happens if you find out the costs for construction and renovation are more than you originally estimated?

- What is your exit plan or the fall back plan if the property doesn't sell on time?

- Would you be able to qualify for a conventional mortgage if the property doesn't sell and has to stay on the market?

These are just a few of the questions that you are going to hear from the bank. Remember that there are a lot of people who want to make money in real estate by flipping houses, but most don't take the time to research and learn before jumping in. they easily get over their heads and then default on the loan because they made a bad investment. It is up to you to show the bank that you are serious about this investment, that you have a plan, and that you are going to be able to pay the loan back.

Chapter 6: Choosing the Property You Want to Flip and Make a Profit From

Now it is time to get into the actual purchase of the property you are interested in flipping. This is an exciting time, but make sure you leave your emotions at the door. This will help you to make smart decisions about the property and can make it easier to actually make money in the process.

Investing in real estate, whether you want to flip the property or own it, can be very similar. You should never just jump at the first property that comes on the market that has a good price. You need to take your time and analyze as many properties as you are able to find. Even if you only end up making an offer on one property out of 20 or 30 or 40 properties, this is still a much better idea than just jumping on the first one you see and then ending up with a flop.

Buying a house that you want to property flip and sell quickly is going to be a different experience compared to purchasing a house for your family. When you purchase a personal house, you will see it as a place for the future, a place to build a family and to follow your dreams. But when you purchase an investment property, it is all about the bottom line and how much money you can make. When doing this, you need to leave your emotions at the door and never get attached to the property.

As soon as you get attached, things can go downhill. You will overlook some major flaws with the property, ones that should send a red flag out to you to avoid. You will put too much money into it, not fix up the right things, and end up spending way more than what you could ever dream to get out of the property. Getting involved with this investment emotionally is a quick way to separate yourself from your money and any future profits you hope to earn.

To start, we are going to take a look at the three essential rules that you should follow when looking for a property to invest in. These rules are not in place to ruin all of your fun but to help you to set the right boundaries for your project and to help you get the right one. Before you even try to peek at the property and get hooked on it, you should see if it meets the following guidelines.

It Meets the Requirements of the Buyer

In the previous chapters, you spent some time researching and analyzing the market to learn more about the buyers in your area and what they want and need out of a house. You should have a checklist of must-haves and wants in the house you are going to purchase. As you look at some of the pictures of the house, or even when you are in the house and checking it out, you should physically go through and check off this list as you go. Some of the things you may have on this list (which should always come with you) include:

- The location
- The price list
- How many square feet
- The bedrooms
- The bathrooms
- How many garages
- Does it have a basement
- Is it close to schools?
- Are the furnace, air conditioner and more good?

If this property does meet all of the qualifications that you want out of a house, then there is probably no reason for you to fix and flip the house, unless you can get it way below the market value. This list is going to help you to stay on track and get a house that isn't falling apart and too far away. But if it is missing a few things, or if you are able to make it work, then the property is still something to consider. Some examples of how a house may not exactly meet your criteria but can be changed to fit includes:

- Your typical buyer wants a three bedroom, two bath house with somewhere between 1,400 and 2000 square feet. You look at a property that has two bedrooms, 1.5 bath, and 1400 square feet above ground. With a house this big, it either means the rooms are very large or there are additional non-sleeping rooms, such as a dining room or a den. If this is the case, you could convert one of those into a bedroom for hardly anything and then increase the value and the market appeal. Keep this property and move to the next step.

- Your typical buyer is looking for a house that has a 2 car garage. The subject property has the right layout and size requirements, but you see there isn't any garage. You could consider buying it. In this case, you look at the assessor's card and see that the lot is narrow and the house butts up to the property lines on both sides. There isn't room for the garage. In this case, you would move on to a different property rather than purchasing.

- Buyers prefer to have a property that is 30 minutes or less from the major employment centers. You find a property from the 1960s that could have a few remodels and meets the other criteria, but it is 45 minutes outside of town on a road that is unpaved and poor cell service. This is probably a house that you will discard.

Now, this doesn't mean that the properties above are unsalable. There probably are some buyers interested. But since they don't meet the requirements of your buyer, you will probably have to spend too much time renovating and holding onto the property before you got the sale.

Remember that property flipping is a business and you are in it to make as many profits as possible. You have to set firm and hard rules for your property flipping to ensure you get the best deal and to increase your profits.

Learn What the True Market Value of the Property Is

This is a test that you would use for quick flops or properties that will need very few or if any, repairs. If you want to increase your potential profits on a property and reduce your risk, you need to purchase a property that is way below market value. In a real estate market that is active and, most properties will be listed by an agent, this is sometimes challenging. However, if you do negotiate on a private purchase, you must make sure they don't ask for too much. This is where the real estate agent you chose, and your own knowledge about the market can come into play. The more experience you gain, the easier it is to recognize whether a property is listed above, at, or below its true market value.

At this point in the game, we are just trying to "prequalify" the property. While you are studying the market, you and your agent should have access to a database that shows all the recent sales. Make sure to do a search of all the sales in that area over the past twelve months, ones that have similar features to your property. They should have similar age (it can vary by a few years), size (a few square feet difference is fine), bedrooms, baths, basements, garages, and land area. When you have this information, you can run the median and average values off the sales price.

Make sure in this step you go from the actual sales price and not the list price. You can technically list the house for anything you want, but that doesn't mean you will get that amount. In a market with lots of houses and few buyers, the sale price can be much lower than the asking price. In a market where there are few houses and lots of buyers, the sales price may be above the asking price.

The point of doing this is to check how much you think you can get for the property. If it is listed at $100,000, and other properties on the market are selling for $125,000, you may be able to get the latter value. But then you can figure out how much it will cost to renovate the house. If it only costs you $10,000 to fix up, then you can walk away with $15,000 in profit. But if that house takes $30,000 to renovate, then you will lose money if you purchase it.

Another thing you can do here is use the 70 percent rule. This is a test that you would use for fix and flips or any properties that are going to need some renovations or some substantial repairs. This is a rule that a lot of flippers have been using for years. As long as you have an accurate estimate of the repairs that you will do with this one, this rule is tried and true and can help you make at least 20 percent in profit. The rule is to use this formula when making your purchasing decisions:

(ARV X .70) —Rehab Costs = Maximum Allowable Offer

- ARV: This is the After Repair Value. This is what the property is going to sell for when you do all of your renovations and repairs. You can work with a real estate agent to help you learn this number.

- .70: This is going to be your profit and all the soft costs. This will account for all your costs including any unanticipated expenses, loan fees, mortgage interest, and closing costs. This leaves you with about twenty percent profit margin.

- Rehab costs: This is the amount that you are going to pay for any repairs. Make sure that you include costs for contractors, disposal, and permits.

- Maximum allowable offer: This is the price that you are going to offer the seller. It gives you room to get everything done and still make a profit.

Now that you have an idea of this formula, you need to figure out what repairs need to be completed and the total cost for them. But how are you supposed to do this without looking through the property and getting an estimate from the contractor? This is simply a pre-qualification phase so it is fine to estimate here. When you go and look through the property later, you can determine if the work that needs to be done will be more or less then you estimated.

You can get a good estimate now simply by looking at the pictures of the property. You may not catch everything, but it gives you a little idea of how the property is and what may need to be done on it to make a profit. Some of the things that you should look for in those pictures include:

- How does the kitchen look? Is it pretty dated and will need a lot of work?

- How many baths does it have to bedrooms?

- Can you tell the condition and the type of the floor coverings?

How does the house look on the outside? How is the roof, the siding, or the landscaping?

- Do the comments from the agent reveal any information? Was it a rental?

While this isn't going to give you the exact amount that you need to spend, you will need a contractor to come in to help with this, it can give you a good estimate that will get you started and can save you time when it comes to looking at a property or not.

What is the Seller's Motivation

You can spend all day looking at computations and doing calculations of the property, but unless the seller accepts the offer that you give, you are not going to get very far. You need to know the motivation of the seller to determine if they will take your offer. You will probably be offering quite a bit lower than the asking price and going from there, but the motivation will determine if they accept the offer, if they counteroffer or if they refuse altogether.

Let's take a look at an example of this. The property is listed on the market for $110,000, but you want to offer the seller about 25 percent less than the asking price.

- The property was listed in the past 30 days: This is a lowball offer. It may help you make some income in the process, but if the house has been on the market for 30 days or less, you probably won't get it accepted. The seller just placed the property on the market and they are probably willing to wait around and see if anyone else is interested in giving a better offer.

- The property was listed for 120 days: At this time, the motivation may have changed a bit. The list price may be reasonable, but the seller may be more anxious and frustrated to sell. This is a much better time to bring the offer to the table.

- The property has a recorded Notice of Default. This is where the real motivation comes in. the seller has a house that won't sell and if they don't get an offer soon, the bank is going to take it, and they won't get anything. There is a good chance that the seller will seriously consider your offer and may even take it.

As a property flipper, it is best to start with the oldest active MLS listing first and see what is there before moving to something more recent. This will help you to find the sellers who are the most discouraged and the ones who may be more willing to take your low offers. You can also look at sellers who are not listed and have received a NOD or are going through other time-sensitive life changes and need to sell their houses fast.

The Three Very Important Rules

As a beginner in the market, you are probably really excited to get started and pick out your first property. You may look at these rules and these variables and assume that you can change them around to work for you. But as soon as you do this, you are putting your profits in jeopardy.

In the property flipping world, it is much better for you to be patient and wait for a good investment, rather than rush in and then end up losing $10,000 of your own money in this deal.

You may develop your own style and your own way of doing things as you get in the market. you may change up the requirements that you want for a house or a property because you change up the type of buyer you want. You may even need to change some things because you move to a new market and you find the buyers are a bit different and want different things.

While your overall strategy may change a bit, especially if you stay in the market for a long period of time. But if you follow the three rules that we have in this guidebook, you are going to get the best property for your needs, and you can make a profit on every property that you work on.

A Note About Trulia and Zillow

When you are calculating the ARV, you should stay away from sites like Trulia and Zillow. Yes, there are a lot of sellers who will list through here and it is fine to look through and see if there are any properties that interest you from these listing. But when it comes to ARV, these sites are only giving a general estimate, one that is nowhere near accurate to base your purchase offer from.

In 2012, Redfin conducted a study to see how reliable Zillow and Trulia were. The report stated that these two sites were missing about 20 percent of the active listings in any given market and that it could take more than a week before a new listing was uploaded. In addition, it was estimated that almost 38 percent of the active listings on that site was no longer for sale.

When it comes to an active market, not being able to see a listing for nine days could mean that a great deal for your investing could already be gone by the time you see it on there. In addition, a lot of your time, up to 35 percent, will be wasted on these sites because you are looking at a lot of listings that are no longer available. On top of this, for every 80 houses that you considered, there were another 20 possibilities that never showed up, meaning that you missed out on a lot of opportunities during that time.

Things get even worse when it comes to how well Trulia and Zillow are able to estimate the property value. Zillow does provide a price recommendation or a free estimate, but it is not that accurate to go with this.

According to the Zestimate data accuracy report that is released through Zillow, they estimate that they have a median error rate that is 8.3 percent. And if you keep on reading through the report, they also state that only 38.4 percent of the time are they within 5 percent of the actual sales price. When it comes to the amount of profit that you are able to make on a flip, this margin of error is dangerous and can really put your profits at risk.

When you work in the property flipping business, a mistake that can get up to 30 percent is pretty much suicidal. How are you supposed to come up with accurate figures and make a profit on a house if you end up paying twenty percent too much because your estimate told you that was a good deal? If you follow the Zestimate's price recommendations, you could easily lose all of your profits on every deal.

This is why it is so important to follow the rules that we have in this chapter, and make sure that you actually look at the MLS listing for a property. This does take time and may not be as convenient as you can find with the Zestimate and some other free online tools. But since those online tools are often very inaccurate, it is important for your profits to not follow them. Work with an agent, learn the market, and price competitively.

Purchasing the right property to flip can be an important step to help you get started with an investment. You want to make sure that you are picking out an investment opportunity that is below market value, that won't cost you a lot of money, and that can help you make a good profit in a short amount of time. Following the advice in this guidebook can really help to make this happen.

Chapter 7: The Steps to Purchase Your First Property to Flip

This is the chapter you have been waiting for—the one where we are going to break down the process of actually purchasing a property, going from the offer, to the inspection, and all the way until you close on the property. It is going to be a long one, but it will have the steps you need to know for after you find the perfect property and decide on the property that you want to purchase. Let's take a look a look at the steps you need to take.

The Purchase Agreement

When you are ready to purchase a property, there are two basic types that you will work with. You will either purchase a property through the MLS with a licensed agent, or you will do a for sale by owner or FSBOs. The for sale by owner properties can sometimes be a bit more challenging because you won't have an agent on your side to advocate and work with you. But other than that, the process is the same and you can even use the same purchase agreement.

While some property flippers like the idea of doing the work on their own to save some money for the first few transactions, it may be best to work with a real estate agent to help you find the right properties. A good agent can be worth the extra money and since they are paid by the seller at this point, it is a great option. If you do work with an agent, they are going to have their own purchase agreement so this can save you time.

Once you locate the property you want to purchase, you will fill out the form and submit it over to the buyer's agent, if they have one. If you later decide to step out and make offers on properties that are not listed, you can just use that same form and make copies to use for future offers. Just make sure that all the statements that link back to a licensing authority, any agents, or any real estate companies are taken off. Otherwise, these are state-mandated forms where all legal protection clauses are already put in to protect you.

The Purchase Price

As a property flipper, you will want to pay the lowest possible price on the property. But there are some markets where this can be particularly hard because the demand is so high properties sell at or above the listing price. If this is the case, it may be hard to convince a buyer to even look at your discounted offer in the first place.

This doesn't mean that you should just give up. It simply means that you need to change up your strategy. You can always make a full price offer and then go through a renegotiation later on if you do an inspection that reveals there are a ton of costly problems that you will need to fix.

Safety Clauses

Each purchase agreement that you work with will have a few contingency clauses in them. This allows you to get out of the contract if something is not as expected or if there are some big issues that the seller won't take care of. Some of the clauses that a property flipper should make sure ends up in their purchase agreement includes:

- Subject to inspection: This should automatically be in all purchase agreements, but can be even more important for a property that is a fixer-upper. Though you may already realize the house needs some repair, still get the inspection done. A small kitchen renovation is much easier and less costly to handle, then say rebuilding the foundation. Then, after you get the full inspection done, if you find that there are still too many repairs to do, this is the clause that can let you negotiate a better price, or even back out of the offer.

- Subject to financing: If you do plan to get financing for the project, then you need to get the pre-approval before you submit an offer on a property. But if you are going through purchasing the property and then you are denied the loan for some reason, this is how you get out of the agreement.

- Subject to appraisal: If you put in an offer that is substantially below what you believe is market value, then this clause is not necessary. But if you believe that you are able to do a quick flip, you will want to add this in. Bring in an appraiser and make extra sure that you aren't paying too much on the house.

Remember that the fewer contingencies you add into the purchase agreement, the more likely the seller will accept them. In addition, many sellers do not want to pay your closing costs and they rarely accept offers that are contingent on the sale of another property. This shouldn't be too big of a deal if you are just using this as an investment property.

Earnest Money Deposit

After the seller accepts the offer that you send in, you will need to pay some sort of earnest money deposit. The amount is going to vary, but it proves to the seller that you are a serious buyer. These deposits are going to be held by a third party and will not be released over to the seller until closing. Then this deposit can be applied to the purchase price.

While you are working on the purchase agreement, check that it states the earnest money deposit will be paid once the seller accepts. If you write out lots of offers on properties, you don't want to wrap up thousands of dollars on an offer that ends up going nowhere.

The Inspection

Once the seller has accepted the offer that you send over, it is time to do an inspection. The first inspection is going to be when you go and visit the property and look it over. You won't be able to see all of the things that need to be done (this is a job for a professional), but you can get a good idea on some of the fixes that need to be done, what you will replace, and an estimate on what it will cost. Once the offer has been accepted, it is time to inspect the property a lot more closely so you know the amount you will need to pay in renovation work.

Who to Bring

Unless you have a lot of experience and a builder's license for contracting, it is best to bring along a general contractor. Yes, you may have to pay them a bit for their time, but it is worth every penny. This contractor is likely to find a lot of issues that you may have missed and can provide you with a lot of important information about the property.

During this time, hire a house inspector as well. These inspections will cost you between $400 and $600. Unlike the contractor, the inspector is going to look for issues that affect the security or the safety of the house. They look for things like code violations, electrical issues, infestations, mold, plumbing problems and more. This can help you know exactly what you are getting yourself into before paying for the property.

You can also bring your agent along with you. As your contractor goes and makes suggestions on how to improve the property, your agent can provide some help as well. They can gauge how the market will respond to these changes and whether it is actually going to help you increase the market value.

What to Bring

As you go through the inspection, there are a few items that you will want to have on hand. These are going to ensure that you can really see what is going on with the property and if it is a good investment. Some of the things on this list are a bit strange, but they can really help you to get to know the property. Some things to bring to your house inspection include:

- A camera: This can help you to document some of the problems with the house. It is also a good aid for your memory.

- Measuring tape: This can help you know things like how big a room is when you go get estimates on flooring, curtains, and more.

- Flashlight: You will need to spend some time looking through the crawlspaces in the new house, including in the attic, and in dark corners in cabinets.

- Construction level: You never know when you will want to check what is level and what isn't inside the property.

- Binoculars: One option is to climb up on the roof in order to check the shingles, but most people don't want to do that. A set of binoculars will ensure that you can stay at a lower level and still get a good look at the roof.

- Marble: This is one of the best ways to see if a floor is level or if the cabinets in the kitchen were done straight.

Where to Look

When you inspect a property for the first time you should walk through the whole house to get a feel for it. Start on one floor, when you are done, and slowly go through each of the rooms, each closet, and each nook and cranny. Write down everything that seems out of the ordinary or that you want to fix later, and take pictures of everything.

As you are doing an inspection, there are three basic areas that you will need to cover. These include:

- The layout: As you look through the house, remember that buyers are more interested in an open floor plan. There should be a nice flow through the house, or you should see the potential to create one. Never pick out a house that requires you to pass through a bedroom to reach another part of the house.

- Condition: Look at the trim, the tiles, and the carpets. Inspect all of the heating systems, plumbing, and electrical system. These can be expensive for you to replace, and if they need work, you will have to do it before selling.

- Potential: The real money in flipping houses is in converting an ugly house into a beautiful one. You should look behind the bad carpet or the bad paint and envision what you would be able to do with it.

As long as it is structurally sound and doesn't need big things fixed, the uglier the house, the more potential profit.

When You Should Run Away

As a property flipper, you are spending your time looking for unattractive and ugly houses so you can work some magic and make a profit on. But despite this, there are still some properties that are going to be way too much effort and won't make you the profits that you want. There are also some properties that seem good, but once you get the inspection done, it is best to run away. Some of these include:

- Mold: Mold remediation is very expensive. If you purchase a house and the buyer learns that there was a mold problem, even if you already fixed it, this can turn them off. If you find a little mold in a hidden corner of a closet, you can just replace the drywall in that area or clean it up and it's not a big deal. But if mold is found in the walls, then you need to run.

- Termites: If you or the inspector thinks there is an infestation, you should hire a control specialist to figure out how bad the issue is. surface termite damage is not a big deal and you can fix it. But if you find that the termites are attacking some of the structural components of the property, it is time to run.

- Foundation problems: There is no money to be made if you have to jack up the whole house to replace its foundation. Buyers want a foundation that is level and they will not pay for it. Foundation problems can cause ongoing issues in the whole house, even after you fix the issue. The best idea here is to just stay away and leave this to the professionals.

If you finish the inspection and find that there are a lot of surprises that didn't go into the budget, don't automatically assume you can't go for this property. If you have a seller who is highly motivated, then they may be willing to fix the problem on their end or adjust the price to help you out.

Chapter 8: Working on a Quick Flip to Make Money in Property Flipping Today!

Quick flips are the first types of houses we are going to talk about. These are the ones that you will purchase, do some simple renovations to, and then sell within a few months, if not sooner. You want to get these done as quick as possible, with as little work as possible.

Finding the Right Property

The first thing to do here is to find the right property to do a quick flip. If you want to make money off this endeavor, you must find properties at a cheap price. Since most agents are going to price a property at market value to make the most money as possible, it can be hard for you to find a cheap property when looking at an MLS. You may have to spend some time looking around and find your own properties when doing a quick flip. Some of the places you can look at to find a property for a quick flip include:

- For sale by owner

- Ugly properties

- Transitional properties

- Pre-foreclosures

- Retiring landlords

- Highly motivated sellers, such as those who need to move for a job transfer.

These properties need to be ones that need very little amount of work. There is some other reason, other than a house that is ugly or it's falling apart, for why the property is being offered for the low price. In a perfect world, you would purchase the house, add a bit of paint, clean it a bit, and do a bit of staging, and then you can sell it again for a lot more. This is not realistic, but you want to make sure that any property that is purchased in a quick flip doesn't have a ton of work on it, or you will end up losing out on that process.

Change the Look for Cheap

You want to find a property that will be really easy to fix up and increase the value. The less you can spend on the renovations during this time, the better. Properties that look superficially ugly have a lot of potential when it comes to earning a quick dollar.

With these properties, the important parts of the house are in good shape. The roof is good, the appliances are newer, and the furnace and more are in good working order. But the old carpet, old paint, or the lack of curb appeal take away from the value and turn potential buyers away. The perfect quick flip is just going to need a bit of cleaning power and a couple gallons of paint and you will get the look that you want while increasing your potential profits.

With a quick flip, some of the things that you may want to change about the house to get the most profit for the least amount of work include:

- Adding on a fresh coat of paint: If you are going to update the paint job on a property, make sure that you stick with some modern and neutral colors.

- Replace the fixtures: If there is any brass in the house, switch out for silver. If there are globe lights, switch them out for ceiling fans.

- New hardware: You would be amazed at how much the look of a house can change when you add in new hinges, switches, pulls and nobs in the house

- Landscaping: If you are going to change the landscaping, aim to make it low maintenance. Go with shrubs and some hardy flowers that are simple to keep up. Lighting will also create a good impression in the yard.

- A front door that is bright: Many buyers like to have a door that is brightly covered. Use spray paint rather than a brush to speed up the process and save money.

- Make a nice backyard. The backyard can also be important to selling your house. Create a backyard that is safe for kids and really easy to entertain in.

Make Money with Property Flipping Without a Lot of Rehab

When you are doing a quick flip, you want to be able to maximize your return as much as possible. You are not going to have the property off the market very long before you try to resell, and this alone can cut into the profits a bit. You don't want to spend a ton of money on renovations and cut into the profits even more. Luckily, there are a few things that you can do to help make more money with these quick flips.

First, you must make sure that you purchase the house below market value. The surface changes are not going to change value, but they will change perceptions. The appraiser is going to look past the pretty door and the landscaping so the amount the appraisal comes out to will be the same after your work as before. But the buyers won't be that objective. You need to purchase the house for as much below market value as possible. That way, when you sell it, you can sell it at market value and make money.

You also need to reduce your holding period as much as possible. The quicker you can resell that property, the less you will pay in holding costs including utilities, taxes, insurance, and mortgage interest. If you want to really profit from this process, you can try to sell the property yourself and save a bit on the commission to a real estate agent. If you do this, then you should start advertising for a buyer as soon as you waive the purchase contingencies.

If it goes well, you can even let the buyers pick their own paint colors.

The faster you can find a buyer for the property, the better you will do with this investment. In some cases, you may be able to find a buyer before the sale is done, and you can even use the money you get from the buyer to help fund the amount that you purchase the property for. Then, you can fix up the house and have it ready for your buyer.

A quick fix can be a great way to help you make a lot of money on property flipping, but you do have to get it done without a lot of mistakes or a lot of room to breathe. You also need to find a property that is being offered under market value but without a lot of work. This can be a challenge, but as you learn more about the market and you make some connections, you are going to be able to find these properties and make some good money.

Chapter 9: Doing Property Flipping with a Renovation Property

While there are times when you will do a quick fix, these are rarer. It is hard to find a house that is being offered for below market value that doesn't need a ton of renovations. In most cases, you are going to work on properties that need more time and more work. These properties are going to need varying degrees of rehabs, renovation, or repairs in order to maximize their resale value the renovation can take more planning and skills compared to others, but if you can do them effectively and with as little cost as possible, it can provide you with a ton of satisfaction and money.

How to Find One of These Properties

The challenge here is to find the property that you can renovate and make money on. There are some properties that will lend themselves to this kind of flip better than others. Some places you can focus your attention on to do this type of flip include:

- Fixer-uppers
- Estate sales
- Divorce
- Auction properties
- Multi-family conversions
- Stalled construction
- Abandoned houses
- Transitional properties

You need to go through a lot of different avenues in order to get these properties. Depending on how the market is going, it can be hard. You may need to wait for some time to find these properties, and you may need to ask around to those you know. Networking can be a very powerful tool, and having a good network of those who are on the lookout for you and who will work with you when they hear about a property, can really make a big difference.

How to Determine How Profitable the Property Will Be

When you get into property flipping, it is important to concentrate on the profits that you can make with this endeavor. No one wants to just throw money away and fail when they get into this, so you want to make sure that you have a good plan in place that will help you determine how profitable each property will be before you get started. profitability is going to be a combination of purchase price, holding costs, accurate renovation estimates, and your desired profit. We discussed this a bit before, but the formula that you can use to determine the profitability of a property includes:

(ARB X .70) —Rehab Costs = Maximum Allowable Offer

The Purchase Price

All of this is going to start with your purchase price. If you end up paying too much by five to ten percent, that is the amount that is going to be cut out of any profits you earn on this process. So, how do you know whether or not you are going to purchase a property for a fair price?

This is where your network is going to be really valuable. It is not a matter of getting just the SMA from your agent, but you will also need to work with a contractor to figure out how much the renovations will be. Sure, you may find that the property is worth $185,000, but if you find out that you need to replace the whole roof, you may have to reconsider how much you will pay.

The Rehab

While the price you pay for that property is so important, you also want to have a good estimate on how much the renovations and rehab will be for your project. Remember that renovations will never go as smoothly as you hope, even after being in the industry for some time. If you want to play it safe, get a written estimate and then add on five percent to it to help you be safe. If it is possible to get the work done for less, then you get to keep the extra profit. But if things do get complicated, then you will have a cushion to rely on.

In some cases, you may have to decide which types of renovations are the most important to get done. You may not have the money to do all of the things that the house needs in the time you have. There are a few types of renovations that you should consider doing if you can to help improve the value of the house. The top five renovations that you can do on your property, going in order of demand, include:

- The kitchen: This doesn't mean that you have to drop $25,000 to $50,000 in order to renovate the kitchen. You could consider resurfacing the cabinets, changing a few countertops and put down some new flooring and you can make the kitchen look as good as new.

- Baths: New fixtures, fresh colors, and new flooring can really change the look for your bathroom and make it more appealing to your potential buyer.

- Open floor plan: While older houses can be great for property flipping, often they will be claustrophobic. Taking out a non-load bearing wall to open up the living area can make a big difference to the house and how well you can sell it, without costing a lot of money.

- Curb appeal and landscaping: First impressions are so important when you want to keep the yard green and well-trimmed. You can clean out the gutters and the siding, repaint the doors, and replace the garage door. You may even want to add in some new flowers and shrubs to give the house a better look.

- Flooring: Having an old ratty flooring in the house can date it. You may want to move from vinyl to tile or carpet to wood which can really help move that house up to a higher price level.

There are other options that you can consider doing if you have the money to do it and still make a profit. You could add in some extra bathrooms or bedrooms. You can convert an attic or a garage. Adding in some things for a master suite can really help increase the value you can sell the property for. You have to determine how much you have to spend, how much you can sell the house for, and how much time you have.

The After Repair Value

This is not the point to just make guesses. You need to talk to the contractor about the things they recommend to help with the property and get those estimates down in writing to make them firm. Then take these estimates over to your real estate agent. You need to know if spending $15,000 on the kitchen is going to pay you back the $15,000 and earn you $3,000 or 20 percent. In some cases, it will, in others it won't so you need to make sure that it is worth your time.

When you get your after repair value, treat this number like gospel. Don't try to edge it up or alter it as well. Don't say things like "Oh don't worry. I'll just ask $5000 more. We'll get it, I'm sure." This means that you are walking on thin ice and it's the main reason that these flippers will fail. You should stick with that original ARV. There may be times when you can sell the house for more than the ARV, but it is better to stick with it and earn more in profits than inch your ARV up and not make any profit.

Doing it Yourself or Hiring a Contractor

It may sound appealing to do all the work on your own. Perhaps you have done some of the repairs on your own house and you feel that you have enough skills to get the work done. And you think about all of the money that you could save if you don't have to hand money over to the contractor.

However, this doesn't mean that you should do all of the work on your own. There is a big difference between some simple repairs in your own house compared to remodeling a house that you want to market and sell in a few short weeks. If you are not a professional, you may overlook some small mistakes, but the buyer, and their inspectors, will not and it could end up costing you down the line.

Remember that regardless whether you hire your own inspector or not, buyers will bring along their own house inspector. A botched job is going to be found out by the inspector and could cost you the deal. Depending on what is done wrong, it could even lower the price that you can ask for the house. And in some cases, the work that you need to be done will need permits and a licensed professional doing it. If this happens, you need to have a professional, rather than doing the work on your own.

In most cases, it is best for you to hire a contractor in order to do the work for you, especially in any job that needs perfection and accuracy. They can make sure that it gets done the right way. You can do some of the work and save money, such as the landscaping or repainting the rooms, if you want to.

Some of the things that you can focus on when trying to decide whether or not you want to hire a professional contractor to do the work or if you want to do it on your own include:

- Do you still have a job that you do full-time and plan to maintain that job while you are doing the property flip?

- Do you really feel like spending all your free time and your weekends for six months or more, working on the house and hoping you get it all right and hoping it saves you money?

- Would you be able to afford to do these repairs if you quit your job now and then focus on this project?

Contractors are preferable in most situations. No one really wants to spend their free time repairing the house. They want to get it done right. And often, investors are going to have other jobs that they still have to do during the day. contractors are also used to working on a deadline and can get the work done quickly, helping you get the house back on the market in no time. Remember, the quicker you are able to get the project done and on the market, the quicker you can make a profit.

How to Manage Your Rehab

When you are working on a renovation or a rehab for your property, remember that time is money. The longer the property is in your hands, the more it is going to cost you and the lower profit you will get. You will have to pay taxes, utilities, mortgage interest and more for each month you own the house. You must make sure that your contractors are staying on track and getting the work done on time.

There are other tasks that you will need to manage during this time. You will need to pay any bills on the property and your budget needs to be maintained as well. You need to keep your contractors and any desire that you have to upgrade the house reigned in so that it stays on budget. The minute that you start overbuilding or upgrading and it exceeds what the market will tolerate, remember that you are cutting into your profit margins.

Staying organized can be the most important thing when you are working on this project. As you get close to finishing up this project, keep things on track. You can even create a to-do list that has a final punch list of all the things that the contractor needs to finish and that you don't want them to forget to get the project done.

In most cases, you are going to work on some kind of renovation when you purchase a property to flip. These are the ones that are often under market value, so you have some potential to fix them up and bring them back to the market value in no time. You just need to fully understand the market, pick out the right price to pay, get all the renovations done for a good price, and then get the house listed and sold in a short period of time.

Chapter 10: How to Sell Your Property and Make a Profit

Once your property is fixed up, and even before it is all done, you will need to work on finding a buyer for the property as quickly as possible. This will ensure that you are able to get the house off the market and sold, bringing you as much profit as possible. Selling the property can prove to be another challenge as well. The price needs to be right, the renovations and fixes that you did need to impress, and you need to advertise to the right people. Let's take a look at some of the steps that come with selling your property flip.

Selling on Your Own or Selling with an Agent?

Buying a property using a real estate agent is a great idea. The seller is the one responsible for paying the commission for that agent, so you get all the benefits of using an agent without having to pay for any of it.

However, when it comes to selling the property, the services, assistance, and experience of an agent can be useful, but they do come with a price which can eat into your profits.

Paying commission to the real estate agent can be a significant expense that you need to factor in to help you figure out your profits. When you multiplied your ARV by the .70, the commission that you will pay to the agent is automatically figured in as part of the 30 percent profit margin. Most real estate agents are going to charge between 5 to 7 percent of the sales price. So if you sell a house for $250,000, you would have to pay the real estate agent between $12,500 and $17,500. A real estate agent can be worth the cost, but you have to remember that when you think about your profits.

The real estate agent will do wonders to help you sell your property, so writing them off just because of the expense is a bad idea. They will help you find a buyer. They will take care of any and all costs for marketing your property. They will be the ones who show interested parties the house. They will work with the agency who is handling the closing to make sure it is all done right. If there are any complications in these areas, the agent will step up and try to resolve them.

This can be nice for you. Instead of focusing so much on reselling the house after you did all the renovations and rehab, you can work on finding the next investment. Plus, you have to seriously consider whether you have the skills and resources in order to do the selling on your own. Real estate transactions have a lot of variables and doing it on your own can risk a lawsuit from a buyer who isn't satisfied. Having an agent with the right credentials can reduce the likelihood that something like this is going to happen, and they can take a lot of the work off your plate.

With all that in mind, it is often best that for the first couple of properties, it may be nice to have an agent. They will be able to help you to get used to the whole process and at least learn the ropes before you decide to do it all on your own.

Attracting Buyers to Your House

With property flipping, the faster you are able to locate a buyer and close the deal, the better. You want to find buyers who are going to pick your property over any of the other similar options on the market. some of the things that you can consider doing to help make your investment property stand above the rest include:

Advertising

When you are ready to sell your property, you need to start advertising it. If you work with a real estate agent, they will take care of the advertising for you, saving you a lot of time and hassle. But if you are doing the advertising on your own, you may need to start early. In fact, consider starting before the property is completely ready for the market so you can get potential buyers lined up and ready to go.

There are many different places to list your property. You can list in the local classifieds. You can use some of the social media sites for your area. You can even work with some options like Zillow and Trulia. While these options are horrible when you are trying to use them for estimates on the value of a property, they can be a good way to reach your potential buyer and get them to contact you about the property.

Whether you use a real estate agent or not, it is important to start networking with others in your community. This will help you spread the word about each of your properties. Just because someone in your network doesn't need the property right at that time, doesn't mean they won't need a property you have later on, or that they don't know someone who is searching right now. This can prove to be a great resource for you as you continue to grow this business.

Staging

Sometimes, buyers are not going to have the vision to see the full potential of the house. They may need a bit of encouragement to envision just how the house will look when it is furnished. Often, leaving the rooms empty can really turn off a potential buyer. A house that is well-staged will sell way faster than a house that is left vacant, even if the buyer doesn't end up keeping some of the furnishings.

There are three options you can choose from when you decide to do staging. You can choose to do it yourself, do a rent to own type of company, or use professional stagers. If you want to sell a mid to high range house, a professional stager can be worth the extra cost. You could even rent a living room and master bedroom set if you need and then return the items when the house sells. You can do the work yourself if you feel confident in your abilities and want to save a little money on this step.

Open Houses

While there should be buyers who will contact you to do private viewings of the house, open houses can have some value as well. This is a great way to show the community all the improvements that you did on the property. Make sure that you have plenty of before and after pictures for them to look at and that there are some business cards and flyers available. You probably won't sell the house from that open house (although it does happen sometimes), but you can get a referral to a buyer who might.

Land Contracts and Lease Options

One surprising fact you may run into is that there are a lot of buyers who have a decent credit score, but they don't have enough money to come up with a down payment to get their loan. If you do a background check or a credit report on the buyer and you find that they are low risk, you could consider selling the house on a land contract or lease option.

There are a few problems that can prop up with this one though. First, you are going to lock up your capital for the next year or two. But the additional payments and the interest that the buyer gives you can actually increase your return.

The lease option is going to have two documents that are important. One is going to be for the lease and the other one is for the purchase. The renter is going to pay a market rate of rent, plus a monthly payment for the future purchase of the house. If they end up backing out of the lease option or can't make the payments, then you get the house back to sell, and all the payments they already made are non-refundable.

You can also choose to go with the option of selling the property on a land contract. The down payment for this one is going to be lower than other options, staying under ten percent. But the interest rate here is going to be much higher than some conventional loans. After three to five years, the buyer will need to pay off the loan so that your capital is freed up.

These two options are often saved for a last resort. They can bring in a little more money than just selling the property outright, but your capital will be tied up for a few years at a minimum and you won't be able to invest in other properties while the money is busy. Most investors choose to not go with this option because it adds in another layer of paperwork and it means they may have to miss out on some potential opportunities in the process.

Selling your house is very important. If your property stays on the market for a long time without anyone giving you an offer, you are not able to make any money and some of your own money will be lost in utilities, interest, taxes, and other things each month that the house sits on the market. Try to get the property listed before you are even done with all the repairs. Closings can take a few months in most cases. If you wait until the property is perfect before even finding a buyer, it means that much more of your profits will go out.

Do I Want to Rent Out My Property?

While this guidebook is about purchasing a property to flip, there may be times when you want to consider renting out the house. For this idea, you may have purchased a property because the market looked good and you were excited about how well the appreciation was going up in that area. Maybe there had been news about a new company moving into the area and offering a ton of jobs. So, you found a property for a good price and got it ready to sell about six months later.

But when you went to sell the property, or during the time that you were working on the property, the market went down. While most markets stay steady for a few years at a time or more, there are times when the market can change in six months. Maybe that new company didn't actually move into town, so the housing market never went up. Maybe the government made a surprise announcement that they were raising interest rates or putting more stringent rules on mortgage lending, so now there are fewer buyers in the market.

For whatever reason, the market that you had entered the property flip on is now gone. You may find that there are very few buyers in the market, or that the price you want to sell the house for is no longer viable. Instead of being stuck with the property or losing money when you try to sell it, consider making it a rental property.

Doing this can help you recover some of the expenses and can even earn you an income. You can charge a market rate of rent that will help cover your mortgage and pay off a little extra at a time. You can get the mortgage rate down a little bit more as well, allowing you to build up more equity in the process, or to help you to make more profits when you do decide to sell the property.

After a year or two, the market in your area may be ready to turn around again. When this happens, you can still sell the property. And when the market turns around, you can earn a profit, rather than taking the loss from before. Since you were paying down the mortgage through the rent money from your tenant, you will be able to earn more on the property than before.

This is an option to consider any time that you find the market changes when you are fixing up the property. In most cases, it is not something that you are going to need to worry about since you plan to sell the property quickly after you purchase it. But it is something to remember in case the worst happens and it can greatly reduce the risk you take on with the property.

Chapter 11: Challenges That Come with Your First Property Flip and Beyond

After you have been able to sell your property, you can move on to the next step; enjoying your profits and looking for the next real estate endeavor that you want to take. You can continue on with this process for as long as you want, growing your profits and getting better each time that you go through this process. It can be a very rewarding investment that can keep moving on from one year to the next.

Property flipping can be a profitable business for those who are able to invest in the right properties, stick to a budget, and work hard. But no matter who gets into this kind of investment, there are going to be some challenges that can make property flipping stressful and even risky. Knowing what challenges can come up when you are getting into real estate investing can make it easier to know more what you can expect. Some of the challenges that you may face when you get into real estate investing include:

Your ARV is Always Changing

One of the biggest challenges that you can face when you get started with property flipping is that the ARV is always changing. Flippers who think that they can sell the property for whatever they want and that adding a few thousand to their asking price are going to be in for a big surprise. The market is not that gullible. They know what the fair market price is for a property. Make sure that you get an ARV that is reliable and then stick with that, no matter what happens during your flip.

The Tax Implications

Because you are planning on selling that investment property within your first year of ownership, you won't have to deal with some taxes, such as the capital gains tax. But any of the profit that you make on the sale will be taxed as if it were your ordinary income. Unless you work with a good tax accountant or a tax advisor who can help you set up yourself as the right corporation, you are going to have to report that profit as self-employment income, which can cost you more in the long run.

There are several options in corporations you can consider using based on what protections you want and how much you plan to do with your investment. When it comes to these though, the S-corporation is better than some of the others. These corporations will provide you with more legal protections and tax advantages than other options.

In addition, remember that you will need to pay taxes on any income that you earn during your real estate investing. It is recommended that you set aside about 25 percent of your profits to pay your taxes. You should consider working with a CPA or another accountant during this time as well. They can explain some of the different tax rules that will apply to you and can help you get as many discounts as possible during tax time.

A Lengthy Holding Period

The longer you hold onto the property that you purchased, the more it is going to cost you and the less in profits you are able to earn. Flippers who seem to take their time and drag their feet, either on purpose or because other obligations come up, are going to see a rise in their holding costs, something that slowly eats away at any profits you hope to gain.

In addition, even if you moved through the repairs quickly and did your best to provide the buyer with what they wanted, if you list the property for sale during a time when there just aren't that many buyers on the market, you may have to hold onto the property for longer and pay more in holding costs as well.

It is important that you be aware and careful of all this. If you have the property, move quickly so you can get it on the market and sold when there are a lot of buyers looking for a property. If you can, try to time the construction of the property to happen during the slower times of November to February since there aren't going to be that many buyers on the market at that time anyway. Then, when the springtime comes around and more buyers are ready to look around, list the house as ready to go.

Lack of Experience

If you purchase a property and then do poor quality repairs and renovations, it can end up pulling down the value of your house because buyers are going to see that poor quality as a liability, rather than the upgrade you were intending. While hiring a contractor is going to cost a bit more and will cut into your profits a bit, it is much better to use them when needed. They can do high quality work that will ensure you get the asking price that you want. It may be hard to pay the extra at the time when money is already flowing out like crazy, but it is money that is well spent when it comes to your bottom line.

If you are worried about not having enough experience with the real estate market, then it is time to get some. You can find a mentor in the field, someone who is willing to answer your questions and walk you through the process. You can work with a real estate agency to learn on the go as well. Take any chances that you can to learn the industry and make sure that you learn the industry and can reduce your risks and do a better job when it comes to property flipping.

Not All Property Flips Are Going to Be Profitable

While the steps above may not sound impossible or too difficult even, it is hard to make money in flipping properties. This becomes even harder when the price of appreciation slows down or even reverses. As a property flipper, you are going to assume that the values of properties in your area are going to increase during your holding period, which is so important because it will add to the profits you can earn.

When you are working in a strong market, a lack of foreclosure deals and discounted houses can really reduce the supply and increase the amount of competition among flippers. If you are property flipping in markets that are higher priced, this can be a challenge because it is going to cost so much to get that property in the first place.

Flippers who decide to take on this investment full time can make a good living, but there are issues with cash flow sometimes. When the property is under construction, you are dealing with a constant flow of money leaving, without any coming in. In some cases, it can take six months of renovation bills before you see any income. Flippers have to be able to stay on the market and have a good plan in place to help with repairs.

Chapter 12: Tips That Will Help Reduce Your Risks and Help You Make Maximum Profit on Your Flip

One final note and thing to consider is that if you would like to make sure you maximize your return on the property, you may want to live on the property while renovating. If you were already living in an apartment before, you could move into the house and have that be your whole housing expense until you sell the property. You can spend more time working on the project and your holding costs will also be your living expenses, which can really help you to make more profits in the end. This works the best for singles, but it is something to consider when you start.

Watch Your Time Versus the Money You Make

Your time is very valuable when it comes to real estate investment. Yes, you can make a profit on almost any property that you choose to go with, as long as you did your research and picked a good one. But if you spend months on the property and only make a small profit, then you are going to end up losing money in the process.

Let's look at an example of this. If it takes you six months to work on a property with a full-time rehab, but you only make a profit of $5000, that's not that great. It means that you only earn about $5.20 an hour, which you will make better income in your regular job without all the risk.

However, if you work 20 hours a week for two months and earn the $5000 in profit, you earn $31.25 per hour, which is much better. If you can do 20 hours a week for six months and earn a profit of $20,000, you could earn $41.67 per hour. The length of time may matter in some cases, but it also depends on the work that needs to be done and how much profit you believe you are going to make from that work. If you can earn a large profit from working a little longer, then go ahead and do it. But don't shuffle your feet on small work that will barely earn you any money at all.

Make Sure That You Don't Run out of Money

If you run out of money on the project, you are going to end up having to stall the project and you will lose more money. This is something that is going to happen to beginners. They assumed the project would only take a month or two, when in reality, that type of project takes six months. They assumed that things wouldn't cost as much as it did. They didn't budget enough. They decided that they wanted to go with all of the upgrades.

This is why you want to make sure that you go through and create a budget before you start, and make sure everything is accounted for. If you aren't sure what needs to be in this budget, then find someone to discuss this with, such as a real estate agent or someone else who works with house flipping as their investment as well.

If you are worried about running out of money during this process, consider overestimating how much you need. You can add five to ten percent to the amount that you plan to need for the whole project. That way, if the project takes longer than expected, or if you have to hold onto the room a bit longer because it takes a bit to sell it, then you are all covered and won't have to stall the whole project.

Under Build Rather Than Overbuild

When you get into a new house, you may be excited about all the potential that is there. You may want to add things in, take things out, and really make some changes. This is great that you have a lot of vision with the project, you do need to be a bit careful. If you spend too much time overbuilding the project, you will end up spending too much money and you won't earn it back in the profits you earn on the property.

For example, while a bathroom and kitchen are important for selling the house, and it will be almost impossible to sell the house if you don't make sure that these are as updated and nice as possible, you have to keep the costs down. While these two areas of the house are vital to the sell the house, a complete remodel of one or both will rarely bring you enough to cover the costs.

Instead of doing the full repair or renovation in these areas, see what little changes you can do to help get them to look nicer. Replacing a few appliances, changing the color, and changing the floor a bit can often go a long way in helping you to get those areas fixed and ready for the buyer, without costing too much out of pocket.

Remember to Factor in Those Holding Costs

Investors remember to put in the cost of the house. They remember to factor in how much it will cost to pay the real estate agent. They remember to factor in all repairs and any costs that they put in for advertising and more. But one thing they always seem to forget about is the holding costs. These are very real costs that can eat into your profits, and if you don't factor them in, especially if you hold onto the property for many months, you are going to end up with no profits at all.

There are various things that are going to be included in the holding costs that you have. They can include things like utilities, interest on the property, taxes, house-owner's association fees, and more. These are the costs that are going to be necessary to keep the property, and they can quickly add up the longer you own the house. When you factor in the costs and how much you will have to spend on the property, remember that you need to factor in these holding costs so you can an accurate profit amount.

Choose the Property That Is the Best Investment, Not the First Property You See

As an investor, you need to protect your income as much as possible. This means that you need to know when a property is actually a good investment and will bring you an income, and when a property is just going to cost you money and won't bring in any profits. As a beginner, this can be hard to figure out, which is why it is so important to take things slowly and really do your research before purchasing anything.

Let's look at an example here. If you find a house that looks like a fixer-upper, you will have to take a look at the price and the market value. You find that the asking price is $80,000 and the market value for other similar houses seems to be about $135,000. This may seem like a great deal because you have the potential to make $55,000 in profit if everything goes well.

After you purchase the house, you find out that there is a lot of work that needs to be done. You need to replace the foundation, you have a mold problem, the furnace needs replaced, there is radon in the basement, and the roof needs new shingles. In all, you end up spending $40,000 on these repairs. That's not such a big deal, you still have some profits.

But then you go to the market and find out that the market price of the house is $130,000 instead. Then you used a real estate agent and need to pay for their commission. Add on your holding costs and more, and now you end up with $145,000 spent on a house you can only earn $130,000 on. This is a great example of how just because a house is listed at a price that looks nice doesn't mean that it is the right option for you to choose.

Do Not Try to Take on More Risk Than You Can Bear

Each property that you look at is going to have different levels of risk. Some properties simply need a little paint and some updated appliance and you are ready to flip the house. Maybe an older couple who had lived there for fifty years were finally moving to Florida to enjoy their retirement, and they just want the property off their hands as quickly as possible. You could get a great price (the couple paid the house off years ago and are happy to pocket the profits) without having to do a ton of work if the couple properly maintained the house.

But many times, the property can go the other way. There is usually a good reason that a property is being offered for such a good price, and that reason is that the property needs a ton of work done to it.

To make money with real estate investing, you are going to have to put in some time and sweat. Or you are going to have to pay someone else to do that for you. But the amount of time and sweat and even money that you put into the project is going to depend on how much risk you are willing to take.

You will probably have a different risk tolerance than someone else. You may see a fixer-upper that is in bad shape and be excited to see how much you can get the house for, how much work you can get done on a dime, and more. You like the challenge. But for beginners, this can be too much, and it may be better to start out with something that won't carry as much risk, or as much work, at least for the first few properties.

Develop Your Own System

This guidebook took a lot of time to explore some of the steps that you need to take in order to get your property flip done. We looked at how you can look for houses, how to make a purchase, how to get the repairs done, how to sell the house, and so much more. These are some simple steps that you will really see success with, but it is still important for you to take the time and come up with a strategy or a process that works the best for you.

Before you get into any real estate investment, take the time to write out your process step by step. Use the same suppliers, the same materials, and the same paint colors when you can. Even try to stay with the same timeline on each project if you are able to. Not only will it make the process much easier, it can also reduce your stress and helps you to calculate expenses and profits on each flip you do.

Be Patient

Professionals are going to take their time. They know that there is a lot of money on the line; potential money that could come in if they pick the right property and make a profit, but also potential money lost if they choose wrong. Professionals are not going to just jump on the first property that they see.

Novices often will purchase the first fixer-upper they find and then hire a cheap contractor to get the work done. But this can backfire. The property may be in a bad location, the contractor may never show up or do bad work. The novice may hold onto the property for a long time before even being able to sell it. And because the work on it was done so poorly, no one is willing to pay the asking price and the novice walks away with little to no profit. And in some cases, they have to take a big loss on their work.

As a professional, you do not want this to happen. You want to take your time to find the perfect property, the one that is going to help you to make a big profit with as little work as possible. It may be frustrating, but sometimes this takes a bit to accomplish. Keep doing your research and keep watching the market. the right property will show up in time, and you will be so glad that you waited it all out.

Try to Sell the House on Your Own

This one can really help to cut out some of the commissions that you have to pay. Real estate agents can be nice to make the work easier and to save you some time, but their commissions can be large and will really eat into your profits. If you do a property and have to handle the costs and the repairs, and then you have to add on another $10,000 or more to pay the real estate agent, it is harder and harder to find a good property that will actually make you money.

While some investors will choose to work with an agent, and you might consider this as well during your first few properties, if you want to save on commission, and also open up more properties that you can invest in, then you need to try and sell the house on your own. This is something that many sellers have done in the past, even individuals who are looking to sell their own personal houses before moving.

You have to have some patience to get this done though. You need to advertise as quickly as possible, preferably before the property is even done with the renovations. You need to be there to show the house and to do open houses. And you have to be ready to negotiate on the price with any potential buyer. But if you can put in a little bit of work with this one, and you price your house at a competitive price, you can easily do this work on your own and save a bit of money.

Make Your Estimates for Repairs Higher Than You Think

Repairs on a property flip never go the way that you plan. Even if you get a written estimate on the project, there may be some added expenses that come up while the renovations are being done. And some of these have to be fixed because they are substantial and will affect how the buyer perceives your house and whether they will purchase the property or not.

When you are figuring out all of your numbers to see if the property is a good one to invest in, make sure to estimate the costs of repairs a little bit higher. So, if you get a bid for all the work in the property, add five percent to it. In some cases, the renovations will come in at cost, and you simply get to take that five percent and add it into your profits. But for those times when everything doesn't go the way that you planned, at least you have some cushion in place to get it taken cared of, rather than scrambling to find that extra money.

Working in real estate investing is a great way to help you to make an income with your own money. There are some risks that show up when you go into this type of investment, and the potential losses can be large, which is why you don't see everyone jumping onto this opportunity. But if you follow the steps that are in this guidebook, and you be careful with reducing your risks as much as possible, you are going to get some amazing results and make a property on your investment in no time.

Chapter 13: A Review of Property Flipping and How to Get Started

The point of this guidebook is to help you better understand some of the basics, and some of the ins and outs of property flipping and real estate investing. If you are looking for a way to work for yourself and you don't mind a little bit of risk and a little bit of working with your hands, then this type of investing can be a very rewarding, and profitable, line of work.

Now that we have spent some time talking about how to get into the real estate market and how to pick the right property, let's break it down into some easy to manage steps that you can take with you later on. You may end up adjusting these steps a little bit once you get going and have your own method. But as a beginner, use this as a type of checklist to help you get going. Here are some of the steps you can take when you are just getting started:

1. Figure out your financing so you can be prepared

a. Save for that down payment. Research some of your options and figure out how much you will need to save.

b. Get your pre-approval. This will make it easier to get your offer accepted and can move the process along faster.

c. Figure out how you are going to pay for the repairs. Some loans will cover this for you, but make sure you know how you will do it.

2. Partner with a good real estate agent. This person can be invaluable to you. They provide you with information on the market, can help you figure out the average of houses in your range, and can even help you find the right properties when you are a buyer.

3. Find a contractor. They will help you to get the work done quickly and ensure that it is high-quality.

4. Find 20 houses. You may not use all of them (and in most cases, you will only use one or two at most),

but it at least lets you know what is out there. Some of the places where you can look for these houses include:

   a. MLS

   b. Notice of defaults

   c. Non-listed properties that are run down.

   d. FSBOs

5. Analyze all of the properties. This will help you to know which properties will actually cut it and help you make a profit.

   a. Analyze the property

   b. Study the market

   c. Determine the wants and needs of the buyer. Then look to see if the property has these, or is at least have the ability to be turned into what the buyer wants and needs.

6. Make an offer on the options that are the best. You will probably want to offer for less than what the

seller is asking so you get the best results and you have some room to negotiate. Remember that it is important to look at the way that the seller feels at the time, and if they just listed the property or if they really need to sell it. This will make a difference in how much you offer.

7. After the closing is done. Start to get to work with the repairs. Consider listing the property before they are done to get the buyers in.

    a. Stay on budget

    b. Watch your costs vs. ARV

    c. Do the work as high-quality as you can to impress the buyers.

8. While you get to the end stages of the construction, start marketing the property. This shortens the amount of time that you have the property and can help you increase your profits.

9. Sell the property

10. Repeat these steps to help you keep going with your new investment.

Remember that when you get into real estate investing, it all starts out with one good property. If you can do well with your first property, rehab it, and get it sold, you can use the profits from that one and slide them over to the next investment. This may mean that you won't make a ton of money to use as you want for a while, but it does help your business grow. Your system will improve, your return on investment will compound, and you will find that real estate investing is a great option to go with.

So, if you do anything, really take your time with that first property. It is going to make all of the difference in how this whole business can go. If you can do a good job on that first one, you can continue with this trend and really get your business to grow.

Conclusion

Thanks for making it through to the end of Real Estate Investing—Flipping Houses for Profit. Let's hope it was informative and was able to provide you with all of the tools you need to achieve your goals whatever they may be.

The next step is to go through these steps and get into the real estate market for yourself. What most people don't realize is that real estate investing can take a lot of time, research, and money before you ever realize any of the profits. It's not as lucrative as some may think, especially if you are not careful and you just pick the first property you find.

But if you are willing to put in the hard work and wait for the right property, you will see that real estate investing can make you more money than you ever dreamed of. And this guidebook will ensure that you are setting out on the right trail to make that happen.

www.ingramcontent.com/pod-product-compliance
Ingram Content Group UK Ltd.
Pitfield, Milton Keynes, MK11 3LW, UK
UKHW022226230426